IF IT WERE NOT SO

IF IT WERE NOT SO

"If it were not so I would have told you. I go to prepare a place for you."— John, 14:2

ROY A. BURKHART

COMMUNITY BOOKS, INC.
1320 CAMBRIDGE BLVD.
COLUMBUS 12, OHIO

Dedicated

to

ALL THOSE WHO

FROM THE VANTAGE POINT

OF THE ILLUMINED MOMENTS

BEFORE THEIR REBIRTH

VERIFIED ALL

THAT THIS

BOOK

AFFIRMS

Acknowledgment

ॐ.   ॐ.   ॐ.

All of us have feelings that never quite break into words. To express appreciation for the inspiration that led to the writing of these words is beyond my power. During fourteen years at First Community Church in Columbus, Ohio, I have shared with many individuals and families in searching for the deeper meanings that grow out of life, in finding the indestructible present, in discovering the secret of life now so that we who will listen have no fear for the future. To all of those who have in this way helped me write these pages I express heartfelt appreciation.

In a very definite way I am indebted to Miss Rosemary Weimer, who took dictation of parts of the original draft, and to Mrs. Myra McCrory for creative help in rewriting, in editing and in the final preparation of the manuscript for printing.

R.A.B.

Contents

☙ ☙ ☙

O world, thou choosest not the better part!
It is not wisdom to be only wise,
And on the inward vision close the eyes,
But it is wisdom to believe the heart,
Columbus found a world, and had no chart,
Save one that Faith deciphered in the skies;
To trust the soul's invincible surmise
Was all his science and his only art,
Our knowledge is a torch of smoky pine
That lights the pathway but one step ahead
Across a void of mystery and dread.
Bid, then, the tender light of faith to shine
By which alone the mortal heart is led
Into the thinking of the thought divine.

GEORGE SANTAYANA[1]

A Personal Word

.ल.   .ल.   .ल.

There is the sacrament of that instantaneous moment when one may find a perfect state of being; when he knows no division of time into past, present and future, but when the eternal is his; when the secret of his identity is known to him; when he sees God, if not with his eyes, with his insight, and hears God, if not with his ears, with his understanding. To receive this sacrament is to fulfill life; to know it is to live eternally now, which is forever.

As if we were together in physical presence on a hill facing the skyline beyond, in a wayside restaurant, or in your home by your hearth, let us sit down together for an intimate conversation about this sacrament of the indestructible present.

There is a love that banishes resentment and hate; there is a faith that cancels fear and anxiety; there is an experience of life to be known in the indestructible present so abundant and so everlasting that it frees us from the greatest lie ever planted in the mind of man: that is, that we die.

We live in a universe in which the scientists tell us nothing dies. If nothing dies, we must use a living word to express what happens when the living soul leaves the physical body. What is that living word? Birth! Birth, yes, or rebirth, for man who is born into a physical body is reborn into spiritual awakening and reborn again out of the physical body into life eternal.

To experience the second birth, which is the gift of God's grace, we must hold ourselves receptive, must earnestly seek the secret of life, must learn to have the faith that is reason become courageous. We are born into the life of the spirit as we come to know the Father, who reveals to us that we are His sons and daughters. Coming thus through our Father to a discovery of our own identity, we grow in freedom to love and act on the positive faith without which nothing can be accomplished, and in the freedom to live as brothers and sisters to all God's children.

Only as we develop through the second birth into full growth in the life of the spirit do we prepare ourselves for the third birth. What we achieve in space-time determines our point of beginning beyond space-time. If we achieve heaven in space-time, we are in it when we are reborn out of space-time. No one "dies." There is never an end, but always a new beginning. Man's soul, striving ever upward and onward, moves on out of the physical house that is no longer useful to him. That is all. Heaven is a relationship of union in love with the Father, both directly and through his children in whom He manifests Himself. The slow progress of the coming of the kingdom to the earth is due to man's refusal to respond to the grace that issues in the second birth. Millions of persons in space-time and millions beyond do not know the Father and therefore do not know who they are and that the divine purpose is for them to live as brothers and sisters. And from this refusal come all the problems that haunt the world.

There is no hell except the hell we make for ourselves by denial of the Father and refusal to allow our true nature to manifest itself. Living in the illusion that we are bodies and not mind, giving attention first and sometimes almost exclusively to gratification of instant bodily desires, we lose the larger perspective and constantly suppress, violate, even crucify our true nature, and, in the resultant complexes of frustration, fear and hate, do violence to others who are part of what we ourselves are. If men could only be made to see that their true nature is the good in them and then act fully on that faith, harmony would be established from the smallest to the largest unit of God's kingdom, and peace would prevail throughout the world.

God's love is unlimited, so there must be universal salvation. Each soul must ultimately be freed from its own individual hell and achieve heaven. Therefore there is no reason for man to fear. Instead, he should expend his God-given powers to achieve the fullest possible union here and now, that his task hereafter may not be so great, and that the kingdom may come to the earth before life as we know it on the earth is completely wiped out by the new and terrible weapons of destruction over which man threatens to refuse to maintain control.

To call men to the second birth and its full possibilities is the heart of these pages. Only those who know the second birth become part of the way to the growth of the kingdom, part of the solution instead of part of the problem. They are the co-creators with God of heaven on earth. If you are nearing your third birth, if a loved one is about to be reborn, or if a loved one has in the past taken leave of his earthly house, there is a message here for you. Whether you are in the morning of life, at high noon, or nearing sunset, there is a call here for you. Harken to it that you may help in the fulfillment and thereby be fulfilled.

ROY A. BURKHART

PART ONE

Preface to a Faith

Be not like others sore undone, who keep
Long vigils by the silent dust, and weep.
For my sake turn again to life and smile,
Nerving thy heart and trembling hand to do
Something to comfort weaker hearts than thine.
Complete these dear unfinished tasks of mine,
And I, perchance, may therein comfort you.

> *Found by* DR. LESLIE D. WEATHERHEAD
> *in his mother's Bible.*[2]

Do not come . . .
To sit beside a low green mound,
Or bring the first gay daffodils
Because I love them so,
For I shall not be there.
You cannot find me there.

I will look up at you from the eyes
Of little children;
I will bend to meet you in the swaying boughs
Of bud-thrilled trees,
And caress you with the passionate sweep
Of storm-filled winds;
I will give you strength in your upward tread
Of everlasting hills;
I will cool your tired body in the flow
Of the limpid river;
I will warm your work-glorified hands through the glow
Of the winter fire;
I will soothe you into forgetfulness to the drop, drop
Of the rain on the roof;
I will speak to you out of the rhymes
Of the Masters;
I will dance with you in the lilt
Of the violin,
And make your heart leap with the bursting cadence
Of the organ;
I will flood your soul with the flaming radiance
Of the sunrise,
And bring you peace in the tender rose and gold
Of the after-sunset.

All these have made me happy:
They are a part of me;
I shall become a part of them.

JUANITA DE LONG [3]

CHAPTER I

✑

The Service of Commemoration

IN a universe that conserves all energy nothing dies. So how can we believe that death comes to the highest of all forms of energy, the human soul? What we erroneously call "death" is really rebirth. Consequently, we should no longer say of our loved one, "He died," but rather we should say, "He was reborn,"—born out of his body and out of space-time into full spiritual fellowship with God. He experiences three births: one into the physical body, a second into spiritual awareness, and a third out of the physical body into the fourth dimension.

We will no longer say our loved one is "gone," or that he has "passed away." Where has he gone? Where is where? In the realm of the spirit there is no place. You cannot locate love. Where is love? Love is where people love. God is not in one particular place. He is everywhere. Otherwise he could not be personal to you and to me. God is free from time and free from space; He exists fourth dimensionally, which means that He cannot be located in terms of heighth or breadth or length. God is as free as your thought, as unlimited by time and space as love. In fact God is mind and God is love.

〖 3 〗

We will, therefore, not say a loved one is "gone" but that he is "reborn" out of time and out of space. He is now free as thought, free as love. He has merely abandoned his physical house, but he is here more fully and completely than ever before.

For many years I have had a radio program called The Lighted Window. My body is at one place, but I am in hundreds of homes all over Ohio, eastern Indiana, southern Michigan, southern Ontario, western Pennsylvania, northern Kentucky. Once after a program I had responses from people in three different places in Ohio—one from Liverpool, one from Utica, and one from Pomeroy. I was in all three of those places at the same time, though physically I was in the sanctuary of our church.

Dr. J. B. Rhine of Duke University, who has done research into the nature of thought, now tells us that thought transcends time and space. He even tells us that a mind can influence moving objects, that it has the power of precognition.

The loved one is mind. He is a spirit, and mind is an expression of that spirit. He is, therefore, only "gone" in the sense that his body can no longer be seen. He himself is still here, still wherever he is thought of, still wherever anyone cares about him. The only change is that he is now free from the limitations of the first three dimensions. He has all the freedom of the fourth. He is only limited now by the degree of his illumination.

We think of the person now in new terms. He is not a body, though he had a body. He is not a brain, though he had a brain. A person who lives in his body for seventy years has had at least eight different brains, yet he has somehow retained memory. Some rare capacity has enabled him to hold the images of his entire lifetime. We can count how many brain cells in one cubic inch of brain matter. We can analyze a single brain cell and find out its chemical composition. But exactly what the mind is, that we do not know. All we know is that we are mind and God is mind.

You never saw your loved one even when he lived in space-time. You saw his body, but you *experienced* him. Now you will no longer see his body, but you can still experience him. No one ever saw God, though many have experienced Him. We can see His body, which is the physical universe, but we cannot see God. The body of the loved one was a little universe: it was composed of the same elements that compose the universe or that are found in the light from a distant star.

He has now been reborn out of that physical body which is subject to change into a spiritual body that is incorruptible. This means that you do not think of him as being in a cemetery. His abandoned house is there: in loving tenderness you returned it to the good earth. But you did not put him there. You cannot put a living soul in the ground. It is tragic for anyone to think a loved one is in a cemetery.

Your loved one is with you, closer than ever before; as close as your best thought, as intimate as your most beloved memory of love. You can draw him to you by thinking of him, as you can draw music out of the air with a radio.

You do not say goodbye. When people at a service of memory call out their goodbyes, their terminology, as well as their faith, is confused. To say goodbye is embarrassing. You don't say goodbye to someone who is going to be closer than ever before. You say to him instead, "I love you." You are sensitive and aware. You do not bar him by doubt, or self-pity, or by any thought that keeps him localized in such a spot as a cemetery. To be sensitive to his presence is to invite him and to grow in union with him.

Thinking in this manner, we will no longer linger back with unpleasant events or grief connected with a last illness, as many people do. They revive over and over again an old sorrow. They try to stay in the past, whereas they should grow as their loved one is growing in greater union with God. Your loved one, as theirs, is going onward and upward into greater union with God; so you, too, will want to grow beyond the event of a last illness or the rebirth into greater union with him, with God, and with the God in every man.

At a so-called spiritualist meeting I have witnessed morbid and unhealthy scenes in which people in bondage to an event tried to have it recalled out of the past. On the other hand, I am thinking of a mother and two children who have grown on together after a father's rebirth, almost as well as if the father had continued to be with them physically. They are growing as he is growing, and there is nothing morbid about their home life. They are cheerful and happy.

Some may have known such a quality of union that they simply cannot bring themselves to remarry; but remarriage not only does not invalidate, it actually recommends the first marriage. A wife or husband whose mate has been reborn should not only want to grow onward, but if the opportunity comes should not hesitate to remarry. What finer testimony could there be to the former relationship!

When a loved one has been reborn you will not want a "funeral service." Instead you will want a service of commemoration. For that you will want to plan with your minister.

You will join with your very close friends and others to commemorate the rebirth of the loved one out of his body into the full life of the spirit. You come not because he "died" but because he was reborn; not because life is a dead-end street but because it is a thoroughfare; not because it closes on the twilight but because it opens on an eternal morning. You come together to strengthen your faith, to grow in your capacity for union with God—within your own heart, within the hearts of your friends, and within your loved one.

The service of commemoration should be of a quality to bring inspiration. I have always said that I should like very much to have a choir sing the Hallelujah Chorus at the service that is held for me. People celebrate the birth of a baby. Why should we not feel inspiration when a loved one is born triumphantly out of space-time? While there is a deep sense of loss in not seeing his physical body, we are not losing him. He has now a new freedom, new capacity, new power. Let us hope that we have done everything we could have in the past to help him prepare for this rebirth. But now that he is reborn, let us not bar him by self pity. Let us not be morbid. Let us rejoice in the thought that he is more with us than ever before and that his opportunity to do good is greatly increased.

I prize life in this physical body of mine. I want to achieve the fullest meaning now. I would like all of the years I can have. But when my time comes I shall look forward to it with inspiration. As a friend of mine once said, "When the summons comes I will not be a minute early by my own choice, nor will I be a minute late because of a wiser choice." But when the time comes I hope I shall be ready. I look forward with anticipation to that time because I know that then I shall be as free as thought. I can be in millions of places at once. I can be wherever a parent teaches a child, wherever a boy and girl come to know love, wherever a family is coming to be; I can be wherever young people are facing physical danger and give them protection.

So as we come to the service of commemoration, let us come anticipating inspiration, believing that our faith will strengthen us and that we shall know an experience of love that will leave no place for bitterness.

You may decide to request that no flowers be sent. I believe in giving flowers, but I believe in giving them to people before they are reborn. To give a rose, or a dozen roses, or some other bouquet is a rare thing. If we followed our promptings we would give roses so that every florist would be busy. But when a loved one has been born out of space-time, why not suggest that those who wish to give some witness of love do so by contributing toward some living memorial, as a fitting tribute to a living soul? The thousands of dollars that are spent at some services for flowers that soon wither would do much toward feeding the hungry children of the world, or guiding the neglected children in the community, toward adding meaning to the church building, or improving its facilities for service.

When my mother was born out of her body, we requested that there be no flowers. Later a number of those who had been prompted to give put their money together and bought two vases. Each Sunday morning now flowers are in those vases. I never see them without thinking of her. They are a living memorial.

The nature of the service is very important. Certainly you would not want the casket open during this service. The loved one is no longer in that body. He has been born out of that body. What is there is only his abandoned house. The casket should be closed.

The minister will lead you to become aware of the spiritual presence of the loved one and after that you should no longer look at the abandoned house but keep your heart open to the loved one. In fact, I have requested a plan like this, when the time comes for me: That immediately after I have been born out of my body my eyes be given to an eye bank so that someone who would otherwise not see in this world may have the precious gift of sight; that my body then be taken to its last resting place and returned to the good earth; that if my loved ones wish to have a service of commemoration they have it not in the spirit of mournful regret for the past but of confident anticipation for the future; that they seek to grow in their capacity to experience me and all other people, in the capacity to experience God; that they join together to think about the things that are worthy of the devotion of all of us, to ponder those thoughts that will help them grow in the secret of life and of love.

If you are not willing to accept this plan of service for your loved one, you may at least wish to have the body left outside in the hearse while the service is being conducted, and then go to the cemetery afterwards. If you cannot accept this plan either, then, though the casket is in the room, surely at least you will not have it open during the service nor afterwards.

The service itself might be considered of a threefold nature. First your intimate family may want to have a few moments together with the minister for what is truly your own service.

Secondly, you will join with your friends and those who will want to come and give evidence of their love. That service can be very simple, yet it should be personal.

The service I conduct includes an opening prayer, selections from the Scriptures, such as the 8th Chapter of Romans, the 121st and 23rd Psalms, the 14th chapter of John, and short verses such as, "Thou wilt keep him in perfect peace, whose mind is stayed on Thee." Then follows an intimate talk in which much of the message contained in these conversations is given. Various things are emphasized. Usually some of the qualities that marked the loved one are pointed out, not too

125

vividly, but personally. Then a review is given of who the person is, a reminder that he has not "died" but is reborn. Something of the nature of God is touched upon, and something of the meaning and wonder and mystery of life.

Then follow the closing prayer and the benediction. A favorite benediction of mine that members of our church have found specially sustaining and inspirational is:

> And now may the courage of the early morning's dawning, the strength of the eternal hills and wide open fields and the silent streams, the beauty of the flowered gardens, the love of hearth, the life that is Christ, and the peace of the evening's ending be with you now and forevermore.

The third part of the service is with the family group after the friends have gone and is a dedication of beginning. They are going on. You too, in like circumstances, are going on. You are dedicated to the will to go on and you can be sure of this: there will be the strength, the faith, the support. In fact, if your will is great, you will be amazed with the sustaining.

Do not fear
And do not grieve for me,
. . .
I am like the forest oak
That summer suns have seasoned;
My body will be a little heap of ash
Upon the hearth,
But I shall rise in flame,
In flame that leaps and soars
And seeks the stars.
. . .

JEAN GRIGSBY PAXTON[4]

〖 12 〗

CHAPTER II

✲

Why Now?

THE insistent question asked
by those losing the physical presence of a loved one,
particularly if the loved one was young or at the height
of a productive career, is, "Why did it happen now?"
Often, indeed, from our mortal standpoint rebirth seems
to be untimely. Most individuals to whom the summons
comes are not ready. The instinct to live in the body
is powerful, and very few choose to hasten the date of
their rebirth by suicide. Our great systems of hospitals,
the number of physicians, surgeons, dentists, health
centers, our wide-spread interest in health, all are indi-
cations that this instinct to live, this desire to stay in
space-time as long as possible is universal. It must be
part of our true nature.

Our Father, the Creator, took millions of years to
perfect the creative processes out of which we have
come. He looks upon our earthly bodies as very important. To have us live wisely in them, and to help
us find the secret of life must be a part of His infinite
plan. Man responds to that plan with this desire to
live in the body, and with the infinite yearnings of his
spirit toward growth and enlightenment.

When the rebirth seems untimely, as in the case of a little child or a young person or a man or woman in the prime of life, sorrow is inevitable. Though the rebirth itself is always peaceful—the writer has never seen one that was not—yet the first announcement of the summons is not accepted gladly; and thousands of ordinarily truthful people, who would not think of fabricating about most matters of importance, will do anything to keep a loved one from knowing that the great moment will soon arrive.

"Why now?" they ask, and no answer seems to satisfy. We feel on the one hand that no person is reborn until his last word is spoken and his last deed done, yet it seems to us so frequently that great thoughts were still in the loved one to be expressed and great deeds were still to be done. And when the rebirth was by accident, or due to someone else's wrong choices, we cannot help feeling that perhaps the span was shorter than God intended. We are, however, given the clue to an important distinction in the 121st Psalm, which says God "shall preserve thy soul." Though God created and developed the wonderful mechanism that is the human body, it does seem that in large measure He left it to us to be the keepers of one another's bodies.

The mother takes care of the body of her helpless baby; the sick person places himself trustingly in the doctor's care; the traveler entrusts his life to the clear eye and quick judgment of the railroad engineer; in a real sense each person behind the wheel of an automobile or at the controls of an airplane is a keeper of other people's bodies. Wrong choices will inevitably be made because man's judgment is not perfect, because his attention lapses, because he becomes careless, or because he does not hold himself open to learn as much as he can about life's processes. Some of his choices will result in his or someone else's body becoming incapable of longer service. When this happens it seems to us that God's will must have been broken; yet from our mortal standpoint how can we be sure that all that happens is not part of a larger plan?

As I write this chapter, there is in my thought a young man thirty-three years of age, ready for a brilliant career as a surgeon, yet now struggling with Hodgkin's disease. Is this a tragedy really, or is he summoned to a more than human test? Maybe through him there is an added thrust of the life-force. If he finds the miracle of special healing, as happened in the case of Dr. William Sheldon, then he certainly will not only minister to the bodies of people but his central purpose will be to help them find the secret of life. This testing time may be the occasion for him to receive the sacrament of the instantaneous moment.

The person who found the secret of life as no other has in my fourteen years of ministry at First Community Church was reborn at twenty-one, after facing a vigorous summons in the malady of cancer.

We live in an unfinished world and in a real sense are co-creators with God of this world. We work with His help, and He works through us. How we think and how we live determine in a great measure how long we can live in our bodies; it seems we do not begin to avail ourselves of all the healing resources for body and mind that are in the universe. If we were fully sensitive to them our expectancy of useful life in the physical body would be greatly increased. As it is we make many wrong choices, and when wrong choices are made consequences result that are beyond our control. But God does not will these sorrowful consequences. He suffers with us. And He brings us comfort. Those who have lost the physical presence of a loved one do not mourn long in the intensity of their first grief. Time brings healing and new interests, new loved ones,—not to take the same place, but to fill other places. If we have faith, there is comfort, there is victory. We find the resources to go on and even grow in union with the loved one though we can no longer see or touch his physical house.

We have so much energy to spend, and when it is spent it is spent. But, as Peter Marshall pointed out, life is not measured by its duration but by its donation. We must remember that the one who lived more fully than any other was in his physical body only thirty-three years. He was not hurt; he was not crucified. His body was crucified, but God kept his soul; and who is more alive in the world today than Jesus?

Because we have grown in our knowledge of health of the human body, fewer persons are reborn today as babies than in any other time in history. But when a baby is reborn we must not think that God wants that to happen. When that happens God's will is broken. If the parents have faith they will grow closer to each other. They will have a special representative in the spirit world to keep them seeking and climbing. And the fulfillment that did not come to the baby in space-time will come in the spiritual level. God's will may be broken, but his purpose is always fulfilled.

We must be reminded, too, that there are times when the rebirth seems overdelayed. How often individuals have begged me to pray that they might be reborn! Thousands of people in the sunset of life are impatient for the summons. To them it has been long delayed. I remember one blessed soul who said, "Why doesn't He call me? Doesn't He want me? What is there for me to do?" I answered, "There is some word you still have to speak; some deed you still have to do." She replied, "What can I say or do? Look at me, I'm too old." "You can pray," I told her, "What more important thing could you ever do than pray?" From that day on she prayed for me and for an increasing number of people. When I went out of town she would get my schedule and follow me with her prayers.

I felt the strength of them. In fact the strength of them was in our entire church. Then one afternoon late the summons came very quietly and she answered without a moment's hesitation. It was all very beautiful. Those who cried at her service of memory cried because they had neglected to return her love. They shed tears of guilt, not of sorrow, for all of them knew that though the time of rebirth had seemed overdelayed, in God's wisdom it was perfectly wise.

There is a view of life and of suffering on which we can set our minds to help us on the question of the date of the rebirth. We need to look at the greater wisdom of the Father to come to an understanding of good and evil and the fact of suffering.

We need to remember that the presence of good is as inexplicable as the problem of evil. For several years there comes a drought that sears the land and fields that once grew from green to gold with fruitful harvest; so that they now lie parched and barren. "What kind of God is it who sends such a plague?" we ask. But how many during all the years of bountiful harvest stopped to cry, "Oh, God, the goodness of Thy bounty and the mystery of Thy generosity is past our finding out"? Why do we think beauty and blessings are normal to life but disappointment and tragedy are ruthless intruders? In the same world where there is the ageless wickedness of war, there is also the unfailing love of mothers. On the ship that is driven to crash upon a craggy reef men cry, "Women and children first," and give their bodies bravely to their ocean tombs. If there is selfishness in the world there is also sacrifice. If we say, "We will no longer struggle with the problem of suffering, rather we will give up our belief in God," then we are left to account for all the goodness and heroism, the hopes and dreams and sacrifices of men, as well as for all the beauty with which the Infinite Artist has filled the world.

We must do some thinking about God and His nature. It is all very well for us to say glibly, "God is all powerful; why doesn't He do something? Either He can't stop war, and in that case He is not omnipotent, or He won't stop war, and in that case He is not good."

But let us examine this concept of omnipotence a little more closely.

When God gave to man of His own nature and supplied him with the sublime gift of freedom, God limited Himself. Ever after that there were things He would not do. That wonderful and awful power of choice which makes us men is a gift from God by which He imposes restrictions upon Himself. It is only omnipotence that can grant such a gift. The very limitation God puts upon Himself is evidence of His power, not of His weakness. Think of this matter of stopping war. Man makes war. Every war is against God. Every war is the Calvary of God. Every bullet and shell that is shot opens those old wounds of the One on the cross. War goes on because when the morning stars of human history sang together, God gave man his freedom; sought for a being who by choice would love Him, and so do justly and love mercy. But no one can have the power to choose goodness who has not the power also to choose evil. No race can elect to live like brothers that does not have the power to live like demons.

Then, too, in making a world of law God surrendered power. He limited Himself by the very regularity of the nature that He created. We do not mean that He could not intervene, or that He has not sometimes done so, through the power of higher laws that we cannot understand. But if we are to have an orderly world, it is inevitable that at some points the regularity of nature will defeat and seem to destroy values, as when a child slips on ice or falls over a parapet, or when a helpless pilot feels his plane hurtling to the earth. But let us not forget that if it were not for the regularity of nature, the force of those very same laws through the operation of which some are hurt, no child would ever achieve man's estate, nor any plane ever fly the skies.

The first look at the human scene is always discouraging to the seeker after God. Wickedness is always obvious, obtrusive, clamant. But we must remember that we are not living in a world of exact moral requitals. Speaking of God's infinite love, Jesus said, "He sendeth rain on the just and on the unjust," and then, pleading for the same grace in human souls, he said, "Be ye therefore perfect, even as your Father which is in heaven is perfect." We ought to be glad that this is not a world where evil is immediately punished in kind and where virtue receives its quick and obvious reward. That would be a world without any grace, a world without any generosity or magnanimity. Where would you and I be if a law of exact requital prevailed? if life had never been better to us than we deserved? Surely it would be a world without childhood, because children subsist upon the grace and love of their parents, not upon any meticulous and measured justice. A world of exact moral requital would be a world not of human beings but of calculating machines.

If we had the full story there might be in the Gospels a narrative of a young man who followed Jesus with high hopes and deep dedication, and when at last Jesus was born out of his body, went home dispirited, saying, "It's no use. Nothing but wickedness gets anywhere in the world. If there were any God, surely He would have stood by that Galilaean. In vain I have washed my hands in innocency." Perhaps this young man never lived in his body to hear the sequel to the story of the Cross. Who could have realized in those days soon following, while the Roman legions tramped up the roads of the great empire, that the future was not with them, but with a little Jew named Paul, creeping from ghetto to ghetto in the Graeco-Roman world, preaching the gospel of the One who was crucified?

We find the clue in the 73rd Psalm as to how one man found God's rule and will. Did he suddenly see some dramatic victory of right over wrong? Did he behold the wicked cry out in sackcloth and ashes? Not at all. He says, "I went into the sanctuary of God; then understood I their end," and, suddenly giving lyric expression to his experience of God, "Thou shalt guide me with thy counsel, and afterward receive me to glory. Whom have I in heaven but thee? and there is none upon earth that I desire beside thee." The lesson is plain: the certainty of God's government is not found by observation, but by communion; it comes not by science but by surrender; it is not the knowledge of the laboratory, but the secret of the sanctuary. Those who have been very sure of God have pillared their certainty upon their own soul's fellowship with Him. That is the lesson of Job; that is the testimony of the prophets. Know God by your own dedication to His Holy Will.

There are those who say, "My luck is no good; there is no God." Others, listing all the reasons why they cannot believe in God, say finally, "The climax of it all is war; there cannot be a God if such a horror is permitted." On the other hand, Isaiah and Jeremiah, knowing God, took the opposite view. They would say, "The nations lived for years as though there were no God: see the awful catastrophe that has ensued. What a proof in history of the God of righteousness we know in our own souls!" The one group sees man as a victim; but prophets see him as a violator of the laws of living. That is the difference. And it is plain that the hope for the world is all with the prophetic view. For if, as some conclude, nature, or fate, or some cruel absolute causes war, there is never any chance for peace. We cannot reform the absolute. But if man's sins make war, if God is on the side of peace and justice and the violation of His will results in such awful calamity, then man can, by surrendering to God's sovereign will, know the dawn of hope and peace.[5]

In fact, here is where true religion is the genuine therapy, for the individual, the nation and the whole world. Religion is the experience of finding union with God, and automatically as that union grows the person is either able to solve his problem, or if it is unsolvable, to transcend it, as Jesus did his Cross. He is thus given the grace that means the victory, and this is the only true therapy. If he, achieving union, finds that he has God's nature, his last enemy, which he calls death, ceases to be an enemy, is no longer death, but rebirth out of space-time—freedom beyond space and time in eternal union with God.

I go to prove my soul!
I see my way as birds their trackless way—
I shall arrive! what time, what circuit first,
I ask not: but unless God send his hail
Or blinding fire-balls, sleet, or stifling snow,
In some time—his good time—I shall arrive:
He guides me and the bird.

ROBERT BROWNING,
from *Paracelsus*, Part 1.

CHAPTER III

To Him That Overcometh

DURING the years of my ministry I have only known one family to turn to bitterness. To do this, of course, is weakness. Anyone can be bitter. But that is no solution.

In the case of this particular family, each member entered into himself, becoming an island. Each pulled down the shutters of life, as it were, and began to pity himself. This family could know no comfort. They did not love the loved one. They loved themselves, their own egoes. They had no real thought of the loved one. Their own feelings were all important to them. The dreadful consequences to that family are too painful to be described.

In every other case through these years, after such an event I have seen people grow. The rebirth of a loved one was the occasion for progress in their second birth. I am thinking of a husband and wife whose son was born out of his body very quickly, with no warning. They accepted it with amazing grace. They grew in union with God. They found a deeper union of love with each other. Instead of being the objects of pity, they have become the objects of inspiration.

We can be sure of this: if we have a will to go on, God will give us the grace and the strength. He has not, as we have already shown, promised to keep us from heartbreak and trouble, but there is the assurance of victory to those who believe. To will to go on is to get the grace, to receive the strength, to have the power.

They that mourn shall be comforted. They, however, who pity themselves will know no comfort. They will end up with their miserable selves. They violate their loved one and prove unworthy of his love. Their bitterness blocks him from them. To pity the self is to prove unworthiness. But to mourn is to love. And he who truly loves will discover union and therefore be comforted.

There is an invisible world all about us. We see God's body, but we cannot see God. We experience Him. We see the body of a loved one, but we cannot see him. We are nurtured and sustained by the love of God and the love of His children. We cannot see that love, but it is very real.

You cannot see a family. You see people, but you do not see the family. A family is a quality relationship. If people are a family you cannot see the family, but you can experience it and know it.

There are many roads to an intimate relationship with God. One road is to grow in the kind of insight that will set us free from fear, anxiety and self pity. Another road is good work with our hands, with our heads. Another is doing good to others. Another is giving ourselves and our money and our thoughtfulness. Another is music. Another, the world of ideas. Another, the natural world, with the feel of the good earth, the wind on the face, the sky above, and closeness to all created things. Another is the eyes of a child. Another is the deep union of love. And another is prayer.

To be still in the early morning, at noon and before bedtime, fully receptive and quiet, is to experience the quieting of the mental vibrations so that the real self may be set free and one may know the victory.

The great resources of victory come to us as we think positively. We must know the loved one is here, not gone. He is with us more fully than ever before. We think of others. We center on God, not in our own troubles. He who thinks positively finds the resources either to solve his problems or to transcend them.

If children feel specially the loss of the physical presence of someone near to them, it is important that by act and attitude we reveal hope to them. If we have the will to go on, they will soon catch it also. If they go to the service of commemoration, let us hope that it is constructive and inspirational, and not morbid. We can help them by thinking and speaking of the loved one as present, not as gone. Sometimes it helps children if we just listen to them.

A little boy met a fatal accident one summer when visiting his grandfather. His two brothers were talking one night about it. Their father overheard them. "Why did that happen to Stanley?" one of them asked. And the other answered, "Did anyone ever lend you a pen-

cil for a time, and after a while ask to have it back?"
There was silence, and when the father went into the
room a little later the boys were fast asleep. Thus,
when we are sensitive in our use of terminology and
careful how we reveal our attitudes, we may be helping
our own children meet a time of physical separation.

A child can feel love though he does not see it. A
child soon learns that you cannot locate a thought or
catch one, though a child's thoughts are very real to
him. He soon learns from those about him the thoughtfulness of giving a gift or of doing a favor.

One family that has been unusually triumphant following the rebirth of a father has always impressed the
writer. There are four children in that family. For
years every Friday night they have taken out pictures
and talked about the father, but never morbidly. That
practice has kept the father very real to them. They
have grown up aware of him and perhaps even more
sensitive to the real person than if he had been with
them physically. They have lived in the thought of
him. They have had no sense of his being gone, but
in their awareness have found him very much with
them. In time the mother remarried, but no conflict at
all was created for the children by this new relationship.
One of them said to me, "I now have two fathers. My
first Daddy and my second. But they are both my dad-
dies." That thought was real to this child, and it can
be to others.

In our contact with people whose loved ones have
been reborn out of space-time, we can be helpful in
many ways. We can avoid asking questions that keep

bringing a person back to relive a painful event such as a last illness. Instead of asking questions we can support and sustain. We should help a person look to the future and live for the future. We can uphold him with our prayers. We can get him into activities and relationships. We can be sensitive to the fact that during the first days friends are thoughtful and give evidence of their love, but that later they, perhaps soon absorbed in their own affairs, are apt to leave the lonely person sometimes very lonely indeed. We can by a little thoughtfulness maintain positive contact over a long enough period that the individual can find and master a new way of life.

The secret of victory lies in prayer, in finding union with God within one's own heart and within the hearts of other people, and in being sensitive to the presence of the loved one. Finding the secret thus, one will go on to do the daily work, to fulfill his life, constantly undergirded by a faith that is greater than life itself.

But it is important, as we have already sensed, for us to see that faith is not something abstract. Faith is complete only in works. Belief and doing are inseparable. Faith apart from works is barren. He who believes works. His faith is evidenced in his peace, in his triumph, in his overcoming. His faith is only complete in what he does, how he loves, how he overcomes.

If one turns bitter after a loved one is reborn then he did not love the loved one; he loved himself. If he is beset with anxiety and fear, then he does not believe. If, however, he goes on triumphantly, knowing the loved one is with him, then he has faith. His going on is part of that faith. His enduring is faith. To have perfect faith is to get a perfect answer from the universe.

When we come to the point at which it becomes clear to us that our own time in the physical body is limited, when we are about to hear the summons, we need the faith that will endure. We need a faith that is greater than time-space, one that transcends to the fourth dimension. We need faith that is timely and timeless. We need faith when all goes well; we need faith for the summons.

As this message was coming to its conclusion, the writer visited with a man who soon is to be reborn. He knows it. He anticipates it. He is radiant. He said, "I do not expect it to be different. What I found ten years ago in our church I have now and I shall have then. I found then the present that is indestructible, that is eternal. I shall have it after I am reborn out of my body. While it has grown with me in these last ten years it will continue to grow and I shall seek every means to stimulate its growth."

The experience of this man should be the experience of all of us. Eternal life is not something we achieve in the future; it is the quality of life we find now.

If the summons is due to come soon to one nearest, it is important for us to have faith for his sake, for the state of our faith will be sensed by him. Nothing is more supporting than for a person awaiting the summons to be surrounded by those with perfect faith.

All of which means that it is important for us to grow in faith now, a faith that is full, for then when we face the summons or a loved one faces it we will have that faith to support us. We have the resources. We are sure of the everlasting arms. The sacrament of the instantaneous moment should be eternally ours.

PART TWO

The Perfect Faith

How is it proved?
It isn't proved, you fool; it can't be proved.
How can you prove a victory before
It's won? How can you prove a man who leads
To be a leader worth the following,
Unless you follow to the death, and out
Beyond mere death, which is not anything
But Satan's lie upon eternal life?
Well—God's my leader, and I hold that He
Is good, and strong enough to work His plan
And purpose out to its appointed end.
I walk in crowded streets, where men
And women, mad with lust, loose-lipped, and lewd,
Go promenading down to hell's wide gates;
Yet I have looked into my mother's eyes
And seen the light that never was on sea
Or land, the light of love, pure love and true,
And on that love I bet my life . . .
. . . I bet my life on beauty, truth,
And love! not abstract, but incarnate truth;
Not beauty's passing shadow, but its self,
Its very self made flesh—love realized.
I bet my life on Christ, Christ crucified.

G. A. STUDDERT-KENNEDY.[6]

The continued influence of those departed this life and the sense of reality of the continuing existence of their personalities have been strong enough to remove for me any doubt as to some form of life after death. What it is, or in what form, I care not. I believe that they continue to exist, and I believe that we can be influenced by them.

DEAN DARRACH, formerly of the medical
faculty of Columbia University.[7]

CHAPTER IV

※

Light in the Darkness

WE live in a world of knowledge and in a world of faith. There is a truth that is known; there is a truth that is hinted; there is a truth waiting to be discovered.

Some things we know and can prove. We know that love is the way of life. We know that he who loves God with all his heart, mind and soul, and his neighbor as himself will have a healthy mind in a healthy body, be big enough for creative human relationships, for marriage, for sharing in the important task of building the beloved community locally and over the world.

We know that if we are to find faith in the heart of life we must put faith into life. We know that we must believe in something or it will never be true. Men had to believe they could fly before they could fly. Uncle Sam had to believe he could split the atom or he never could have done it. Men of science must believe that there is the possibility of finding a cure for cancer or they could not carry on the relentless search.

We know that there is a faith that can banish fear and that he who knows it most fully can be used of God to do everything that can possibly be done.

〖 35 〗

We know that selfishness leads not only to illness of body but ultimately to illness of mind. Selfishness makes of a person an island, and he who is apart from the mainland is not well and makes a hell for himself on earth.

We know that basically we only have what we give away in love. Whatever we give in love, we have. We have it not because we give it, but if we give it because we love, then we have it. We know this is a portal to life's secret and the mark of those who have it.

We know that whatever a man sows that he will reap. We know that if a baby is born to two people who love each other truly, that baby will be loving and have the best chance of growing above the cradle stage of self love so that a robust love flows through him out to others.

There is evidence of administration in the universe and there is evidence that it is friendly to men because there is everything here that is necessary for growth of man's body and his fullest becoming as a soul.

We know and I think can prove that the universe is intent on achieving persons who are whole, and is ever seeking to provide that which makes for fellowship. This is observable.

There are some things, however, which I know but cannot prove. I know that man is not a body, though he has one; but I cannot prove it. I know that man has a brain but is a soul with a mind, though this again I cannot prove. I know there is a God. I know that God is personal, and that He is personal to each one of us.

God is mind, else how could we be mind? Otherwise non-mind would create mind. God is kinship. Without that we cannot be whole. God is seeking to help us become aware of our true identity.

I know that what we call death is not death but rebirth. I know that a person has an identity as real after his third birth as before. This I know, though I cannot prove it. I know that a person can grow in spiritual illumination after the third birth. He may be in a state of confusion if he did not know he was to be reborn, but there are all kinds of resources to help him grow in illumination afterwards and each one ultimately does, through help received from those in space-time and from those in the spiritual world, and through resources they receive directly from God. God is within them and they come to discover God.

Communication between those who have gone through the third birth and those in space-time is possible. This I know, even though I cannot prove it. I know that those who grow in a sense of awareness of God begin to find the secret of life and of love; that with all their hearts they wonder how they got along without it before; and that they are restless to have every person find it. This I know.

There are many things you know that you cannot prove. You know if you love someone and that person knows it, but you cannot prove it. You know if you have the quality relationship that is the family, but you cannot prove it. But all those who are a part of that relationship know it.

Yes, there are many things we know that we cannot prove, but being unable to prove them does not invalidate them.

Then there are some things we believe and do not know. I believe that each person ultimately comes through into complete union with God. Only a few people in history seem to have done it in time-space, but I believe that the universe is intent on producing a person who has full union with God. In his book, *The Dawn of Conscience,* Professor Breasted of the University of Chicago, after describing findings from excavations in the valleys of the Nile, the Euphrates, and the Tigris Rivers, comes to the conclusion that the culmination of a developing universe is character. I believe the main intent of the universe is that men should have union with God and that only then is their character sound and their personality what God intends.

I believe in time enough people will find union in space-time, and therefore be free from bondage in space-time, so that men will break away from the ego devotion that makes millions of islands, with resultant inter-group hatreds, exploitations, and wars. Though I do not know it, nor can I prove it, I believe the time will come when heaven and earth will be one.

There are those who say that in thinking of immortality we seek an escape. That I admit. So did Edison seek an escape when he invented the incandescent lamp. He wanted to escape the darkness of the whale oil taper. I seek escape from a thought of life limited between two dates on a tombstone to an experience of life that is timeless. I do not seek escape from life. Those who face life most realistically and want to realize it most fully have faith in life beyond the third birth.

A light beckons us ever onward. The children of Israel journeyed through the wilderness and in Nehemiah we are told that "the pillar of cloud departed not from over them by day, to lead them in the way: neither the pillar of fire by night, to show them light, and the way wherein they should go." No one can deny the wilderness that on-going life will lead us through. That is the bequest of those who lived before us. This life that is never static is a wilderness. Life is pain and disappointment and lonely loss. Life is burden and battle and anguish. Life is ignorance and blunder and defeat. Life is love bereaved, ideals never achieved, gladness soon becoming grief, morning fading quickly into night. Life is a wilderness; it is a mystery. It is a checkerboard of sunshine and shadow. Our Creator compliments us by giving us the task of helping to finish this unfinished world in which we are set.

One of the thrilling things about religion at its best is that it never denies the wilderness. Jesus faced the whole tragedy that is at the heart of life. He plunged into the deepest darkness of the world's pain. All the desperate tides of the world's woe were pressed through the channels of that single soul. Christianity is no escape from tragedy. It is a faith big enough to include tragedy. It is not escape from the darkness; it is confidence even at midnight. Someone who was asked about a jeweled crown which she wore replied, "O, that is the symbol of our faith. You have the cross, but we have the crown." In the religion of Jesus those two are inseparable. Jesus won his crown through embracing suffering, through absorbing into his own love the guilt and sins of the world, through lifting up pain as a precious incense unto God. Jesus went through the night into the eternal morning. He knew sin as no one else ever knew it. He laid his heart beside the world's woeful heartbeat and felt all its throbbing hurt. But Jesus said, "Sin and pain are not the ultimates of life. Death and destiny are not synonymous. The shame of sin, the sorrow of souls, these are temporary frustrations; they do not mark the direction of life's onward sweep. The grave is not an end and a goal. Goodness and not evil; truth and not falsehood; life and not death—these are the positive, all-conquering forces in human experience."

Easter tells us that we are journeying through the wilderness toward the light beyond the skyline. Easter gives us explanation of the enigma of life, insight into the meaning of what seems such a strange medley of experience. Realizing that life is a journey and not a destination gives us more understanding of the wilderness through which we pass. If life is not a goal but a going here on this earth, I may expect its disciplines to minister more to my progress than to my passing pleasure; more to my holiness than to my happiness.

Easter helps the troubled mind become reconciled to all the withheld completions of life. Just when the thinker feels his mind is beginning to penetrate a little into the darkness, the torch of life hisses and sputters and goes out in the night, or seems to. When the saint feels that he has begun to climb a little way toward Christ on the cross, the summons comes. The painter's masterpiece, the sweetest song poet ever sang, these are hardly more than a hint of the beauty that lures the artist's soul. But now the brush must be laid down, and the singer's melody comes fluttering and is gone. In early youth two gave themselves to each other in loving devotion. The years have gone by and each month that love has become purer and more divine, until gradually the two grow into the perfect love which is complete union with the divine in each other. And then the summons comes to one of them.

What is the meaning of it all—these broken promises, these voices that call and keep calling, these hopes that find no fruition, these hungers that are never satisfied? Are they sent to jeer and jibe at us? Are they foundations upon which no cathedrals can be built? Are they ships that shall never sail the seas? If they are then life is not only a mystery, it is a mockery.

Ah, but the answer of faith is, "These are the foregleams of something greater that lies beyond. These are the call to your own completion which is laid up for you on high. We journey through the night toward the light beyond the hill."

In the late afternoon a little boy was building a city out of sand on the sea shore. For a long time he toiled and became so engrossed in his work that he did not see that the hour was getting late, that the wind was growing chill, that the tide was coming in. Then one wave, mightier than the rest, swept in, washing away his houses and streets, his city and outlying farms. Frightened, he started to run. On the bank above, his elder brother had been watching him, thinking how he, too, had once played on the seashore. He reached down and helped the younger lad up the bank, comforting his distress. And through the gathering gloom the two walked together toward the lights that beckoned beyond the hills, where waited rest and refreshment.

So at last it will be for all of us. While we are here in this very interesting interval between our birth into the body and our rebirth out of the body, we have a rare opportunity to discover something of the meaning of life that Easter brings—life that is not measured by the ticking of the clock, life that does not end in the abyss of nothingness, but life that, centered in God, is eternal. Here we can discover some of the great disciplines that face us and challenge us; for God in His wisdom has placed us in an unfinished world. We need no longer be the victims of the things we create. No longer must we cower before the universe in all of its size. No longer do we think we are just bodies. We grow in an awareness of who we are, into a sense of our own destiny, toward fulfillment of God's purpose for us. We grow in love. We grow not only in the mastery of the keys to life's secret, but to the sharing of them with all humanity. And finally when we have finished this interval in our existence, then he who chose to call himself our Brother will lead us beyond the sands and foam of time and place, beyond the curtain, to undertake those other tasks for which life has been both discipline and preparation. And if we find the fullest meaning of life here and now, what lies beyond will not frighten us, but lure us. Though we will love this interval here and find joy in it, give to it and be thrilled by it, learn the secret of it, achieve every richness in it and want all we can of it, we will also ultimately look with eagerness, with anticipation, with faith and love, to what is beyond that great curtain. For the light beyond the skyline ever lures us.

I do not see how there can be any sense of duty, or any reason for altruistic conduct, i.e., any world loyalty, which is entirely divorced from the conviction that personal moral conduct, or what we call goodness, is somehow or other worth while, that there is something in the universe which gives significance and meaning, call it value if you will, to existence, and that no such sense of value can possibly inhere in mere lumps of dead matter interacting according to purely mechanical laws. A purely materialistic philosophy is to me the height of unintelligence. In a recent Fortune *poll, 70 per cent of United States scientists classify themselves definitely as theists.*

Anaxagoras said in 460 B.C., "All has been arranged by mind," and the most influential of modern scientists like Einstein, Eddington, Jeans and Planck have today re-echoed those words of the sage of Athens. Let me close by quoting Einstein's actual words.

"It is enough for me to contemplate the mystery of conscious life perpetuating itself through all eternity, to reflect upon the marvelous structure of the universe, which we can dimly perceive, and to try humbly to comprehend even an infinitesimal part of the intelligence manifested in nature."

I need no better definition of God than that.

ROBERT A. MILLIKAN [8]

[44]

CHAPTER V

❧

Reasons That No Reason Knows

IN our quest for meaning in life, answers come not out of the laboratory, but from the deeper insights of the sanctuary. The fact of immortality can no more be proved than can the fact of a great love. Life is built not contrary to reason but on something higher than reason. It is built on reasons that reason cannot know. We come alive and live to the full only when reason grows courageous and becomes faith.

Faith in life beyond our days persists beyond the logic of time or men; it is a hope that will not down. Sometimes it rises to the majestic heights of luminous conviction, and sometimes it fails to a flickering spark; but it never dies. We are called to a vital consideration of it every time a loved one is reborn, or a celebrity's earthly career closes, and, above all, and most selflessly at Easter. Relentless rationalism does not smother it because it hides itself in the heart of the rationalist; cynical despair cannot kill it, for in the early Easter morning the cynic sees a star and "listening love hears the rustle of a wing."

Whether we doubt or affirm, whether we tread the valley of gloom or tramp the sunlit hills of joy, life keeps burning before our vagrant feet this kindly light of faith that on Easter morning becomes a flaming cross. In the heart of every man is a voiceless question, "If a man die, does he live again?" In the heart of everyone is an answer, sometimes a feeble whisper of a forgotten faith and sometimes the song of the soul's assurance— "Death is not death; it is rebirth! For man was not made to be lost in an abyss of nothingness."

I cannot produce tangible proof of immortality and yet a deep intuition within me persists. Through the years that intuition grows. The last night my mother lived she carried on a conversation with my father who had entered into his immortality while I was in France in the first World War. My mother, a quarter of a century later, ill and in unspeakable pain, had a glorious visit with him; and her only sorrow was that we who sat by her bed could not see or hear him. Just before I gave her the splendid gift of science to dull her pain and give her rest, she said, "John, I'll join you at five in the morning." The nurse called me early the next morning and at five o'clock my mother was reborn in a peace that amazed us and gladdened our hearts. She kept her date with my father. Not proof, you may say, but to the son who witnessed it very strong evidence indeed.

Belief in immortality comes through experience, grows as one grows in the fullness of living, becomes increasingly true as we learn to surrender ourselves to it.

Faith lies at the heart of all living. "Why art thou cast down, O my soul? And why art thou disquieted within me? Hope thou in God . . . who is the health of my countenance." "If I take the wings of the morning, and dwell in the uttermost parts of the sea; even there shall thy hand lead me, and thy right hand shall hold me." But this does not mean that we should ignore the light of reason. Let the fundamental time-tested convictions of the world's wisest have weight with us, maintaining as far as possible the integrity and independence of our own souls. We must leave no steps untaken to furnish our minds as thoroughly as possible, run down every secret we can uncover and discover every reason we can, but we must never forget that reason has its limitations.

A faith greater than life is a faith that we are God's and that God is ours. Look where you will and you will find that faith is everywhere a dominant factor in the fabric and tissue of life. Without faith no enterprise would be or could be undertaken. Faith that the summer suns will follow spring rains leads the gardener to fling his seed away into the moist brown earth. Experience bring him to this act, but he has the faith that his has been a trustworthy experience that will be repeated at least once more. By faith men build their bridges, lift their skyscrapers and send their ships through uncharted seas. They have the faith that the stars will remain in their courses, that the laws of stress and strain will remain constant; they have faith in the continued coherence of steel and concrete. By faith men stake their lives on a belief in God; and that belief does not fail them any more than summer fails to follow spring, or the law of gravitation is set aside for an hour, or a perfect chord of music is harmonious today and dissonant tomorrow.

Yes, life is built on reasons that reason cannot know. Take a human cell, a microscopic speck of living matter—what is it? A whirlwind of billions of electrons, spinning in orbits about 7000 million times in the millionth of a second; and the nerve cells of the brain alone number about nine billions to an inch. Yet look at all of them and you will not see the mind. Dr. Dwight Palmer, of Ohio State University, says: "Touch one of those nerve centers and a person will move his hand and wonder why. There must be some higher level of integration that is the person or the mind." How does the cell become the man? How does the man become conscious of himself? Strange that people withhold faith in God because He is a mystery!

Mystery is all about us. Consequently, life is built on reasons that reason cannot know—faith is at the heart of life. Challenges lie at the heart of life because we go forward on faith rather than certainty. The research doctor does not know, save by the glow of the mind, that he can find the cure; the uncertainty lures him on and gives his quest nobility. The mountain climber does not know if the unscaled mountain can be scaled—the distant peak draws him like a magnet. The boy in this last war did not know that a better world would come of the awful agony, but one said to me: "Never have so many people died for a faith. I must have faith and so I give my best."

Jesus did not know, except in some deep surmise of the soul, that his new strategy of love would win. Others had opposed hate with hate and force with force. Suppose he should meet hate with friendship, force of body with the strength of the spirit, killing with dying love! He did not know, save in burning passion—the unknown beckoned him and he answered in faith. He embarked on a wider ocean than did Columbus. The unknown that puts faith at life's center is always the spur—in medicine, in the mystery of suffering, in building a better world, in the crusade of redeeming love.

We can be thankful for the mystery that makes us build all life on faith, for it calls us to reverence if not to worship. Can a scientist, eye glued to the microscope, watch a cell without emotions akin to awe? This is not the moving of a machine—this is the primal fact of life. Can the astronomer watch the sky without a sense of reverence? Someone has said, "An undevout astronomer is mad." Can anyone watch the miracle of health without being subdued in soul? Can anyone hear great music without being cleansed? Can anyone see Jesus crucified—there he is, pitting his broken body and unbroken love against the venom of man's perversity; there he is, risking oblivion—perhaps none would care or even remember—can anyone see that without being pierced with everlastingness? Even if the great unknown does not lead us to worship, to put out our hand and touch God's face, it will bring us to silence and to ask ourselves the question, "Does Christ still live?"

The unknown that puts faith in the heart of us not only gives life its incentive and leads us to reverence, but it also brings renewal of the soul. It is when we go beyond reason that we find renewal. Faith is higher than reason. Why halt your car to look at a panorama of red oaks? To do so may make you late. But ah, your soul will have a chance to breathe.

There is nothing in the books of logic to justify your letting the faint tremulous note of a violin, or a crushed, faded letter bring back a flood of tender and beautiful memories. But memories as well as hopes have power to bless, and something higher than reason tells us that this is true. There is no good reason why the remembered touch of your baby's hand on your cheek should make you strong in the face of temptation, but some of us know that it can. It is not reasonable to fall upon your knees and lift your soul to God, whose existence you cannot prove; but since the dawn of time men and women have been doing it, and since the dawn of time they have been rising from their knees, calmed and with the flood gates of inner courage mysteriously broken wide open within them.

A young American flyer by the name of Magee who was with the Royal Air Force wrote this poem shortly before he was shot down over the English Channel:

> Oh, I have slipped the surly bonds of earth,
> And danced the skies on laughter-silvered wings;
> Sunward I've climbed and joined the tumbling mirth
> Of sun-split clouds—and done a hundred things
> You have not dreamed of—wheeled and soared and swung
> High in the sunlit silence. Hov'ring there,
> I've chased the shouting wind along, and flung
> My eager craft through footless halls of air,
> Up, up the long, delirious, burning blue
> I've topped the windswept heights with easy grace.
> Where never lark, or even eagle flew;
> And, while with silent, lifting mind I've trod
> The high untrespassed sanctity of space,
> Put out my hand, and touched the face of God.[10]

A boy came into my office and said; "Goodbye, I'm going to take my turn. I'll give my best. I'll try to get back—but if I don't, goodbye for good." I said to him, "You'll get back, whether in a body I can touch or a presence I can feel." He looked at me and said, "Thanks for telling me that, I can do better now."

Another boy, in the thick of it out there, wrote his father and said, "Don't worry about me. I believe in God, in you and mother and in my own immortal soul, and I believe that all that is expected of us in this life is to give our best to others." Belief in God, in parents, in an immortal soul, and in complete loyalty to duty. Isn't that a rather comprehensive faith?

Ringing down the generations is the faith, "Why art thou cast down, O my soul! And why art thou disquieted within me? Hope thou in God." And the thrilling testimony: "If I take the wings of the morning and dwell in the uttermost parts of the sea; even there shall thy hand lead me, and thy right hand shall hold me."

A faith for life—yes. And a faith greater than life. Reasons that no reason can know.

In a world wistful with half-revelations, we keep vigil in our hearts . . . often disappointed, but never losing hope, we are sure of one thing, that the curtain has not yet run up on the last of the world drama; there is more, and that more may come any moment with surprising suddenness. Human life is a symphony, but it is an unfinished symphony, and we are waiting the last movement, the last, or undiscovered chord which will give meaning to the discord at the very moment when it is resolved. There is melody. We cannot hear the birds sing, look into the eyes of a friend, or behold the heroisms and loyalties of men, without knowing there is melody; but it is a broken melody, and "nature slides into semitones, sinks into a minor, blunts into a ninth, and still we wait for the C-major of this life."

Yet always there is a sense of Something very near, trying to lay hands upon us; something seeking to make itself seen and heard and felt. The world aches with the stress of Silence that tries to speak, but is tongue-tied as in sleep, because we do not hear. Here and there a hint, a gleam, of the Eternal bursts through, and as much, or as little, as we see is our religion.

JOSEPH FORT NEWTON [11]

CHAPTER VI

❧

A Symphony of Faith

WHEN a scientist sets up his hypothesis he has reasons. We too have reasons for our assumption that he who lives here lives eternally. But beyond reason, we have faith. No hope is more persistent than our faith in immortality. Like a blind boy flying a kite, we feel the pull of it. "How can you tell it is flying?" someone asked. "I can feel the tug of it," was the reply.

Many of the circumstances of life seem designed to further our pilgrimage, to keep us from settling down, building a home and growing a hedge to hide the restless road. Our loves and friendships grow stale unless we keep adventuring on in faith and devotion; material wealth and sensual satisfactions pall and leave some deep corroding discontent in the soul; at the midmost heart of our pleasures there is some pain of longing. Life seems always to whisper, "Go on, go on," and when we come to life's latest night-fall, still that voice tells of something waiting for us, something which is beyond the horizon. Haven't you heard it—don't you hear it—that unutterable sigh at the hidden heart of life? The certainty of rebirth itself creates a belief in, no less than a need for something transcendent.

〚 53 〛

We have faith in a creative God. We do not believe that creation was accidental. The more we look at the patternfulness of matter, the more we are unable to think that it all just happened. Belief in a Creator is much more reasonable; it integrates the fragments of our experience into a meaningful whole. Disbelief explains nothing and leads nowhere, makes us and all of our thinking dust. To conclude that creation was accidental is complicating. How often would you have to throw up a handful of type until it fell down into one of Shakespeare's plays? The mathematical chance is as slight as the likelihood that some day a kettle full of water placed on the fire will freeze. Nor can we believe that the intricate human body just happened.

I believe there is evidence in the very constituency of matter and the behavior of molecules for belief in a Creator and a creative plan and purpose. I believe, too, that I have experienced the presence of that One in my heart. He seems as real to me as any human I have ever known. I believe He is personal because I am a person; I believe He has the capacity for kinship because I do; I believe He longs for my soul to live eternally because I long for immortality for my loved ones. I cannot feel that He who made us with the capacity to long for immortality is without the power to give us the chance to win the immortality for which we long.

Then, too, we know that in all the world of nature, no energy is ever lost. Light, heat, electricity—all are transferable, but they are indestructible. They may change form but they are never destroyed. Then why should human personality, the highest form of all energy—energy when it has become spirit—be the exception to the law? Why should the lower be conserved and the higher lost? the work endure and the worker perish? the poem live and the poet die? From such a philosophy I turn away. One must either believe that a person is dead when he leaves his physical body, or that he has risen to a higher type of abode—both are faith. As for me, I firmly believe in the validity of the Easter message: He is not here, he is risen. When I knew him he was on the upward way. I saw his love grow more spiritual, his purity more instinctive, his sympathy deeper. He has grown. He is still on the upward way. He has risen. His immortal spirit is trekking with God on the high paths of spiritual development in a future not measured by the tick of a clock.

The world in which we find life's real meanings is the world of personal relationships. Say what we will about the sun, the moon, the marvels of the stellar universe, to wander alone through unpeopled halls would be a dreadful fate, and no creator could so elaborate the cosmic magnificence as to make such a solitary existence tolerable. We love people. That is a major fact about life.

Our love not only enriches emotional attachment, but it strengthens intellectual conviction. Persons are the most marvelous things we know. As someone has pointed out, a falling apple is not so mysterious as the mind that deduced from the fall a universal law that binds the stars together. The heavens may declare the glory of God, but experiencing great souls brings us nearest the divine. Personality is the miracle of the universe, and the mind that understands the stars is far more marvelous than the stars themselves.[12]

Part of the personality we value is transient. A man at seventy years of age has already outlived eight bodies. The brain—its ten thousand cells, its cortex one-sixth of an inch thick, only a cubic-inch of gray matter when freed from tissue and blood vessels—is constantly perishing and constantly being renewed. With every meal it changes, but memory and personality remain. What is the link between the brain and the mind? The enigma is ever debated and ever remains because nobody has been able to catch a thought to cross-examine it. Through all this physical change each person's identity mysteriously abides. You are not your eyes, you own or use your eyes. You are not your brain, you own or use your brain. If you are so unfortunate as to lose an arm or a leg, you yourself are not changed. Part of personality moves in another realm. It is said that Fichte, the philosopher, gave a party to his friends the first time his little son said, "I." Nothing else in the universe except personality says "I." What is this invincible spirit, this mind, this soul, this conscious center of thought, love and purpose that no eye has seen or ever can see? In all my clearest hours my conviction is that this is the real and abiding self of which the body is the transient scaffolding.

Spirit is the real self. Men are not bodies through whose conscious organization transient spiritual aspects, like phosphorescence, accidentally evolve; they are souls temporarily equipped with bodies. This is one of the most vital and important convictions man ever had about his present life, and he will find it confirmed at his rebirth.

Our faith in immortality is manifest in the eternal longings of the human spirit. Deep in the heart of human beings there is a homesickness. Often in the hurly-burly of life we forget it; sometimes in the plenitude of our worldly pleasures and physical satisfactions we cry, "Earth is enough!" Sometimes in dreary disillusionment we say, "One life is sufficient. It is only dreamless sleep I want." But neither mood is long-lasting and neither expresses our deepest honesty. For in the midst of life's brimming joys and its lonely defeats we hear the far-off echo of a bell that stirs within us a nameless longing that makes us sick for home. Our little rationalizations and our weary worldliness never quite silence that mysterious melody.

We have tried to make this world our home. We become engrossed in its work, enamored of its pleasures, consecrated to its need, absorbed in the solution of its problems—but often, if we think at all, we are confronted with the question, "What is it all for?" Most of us spend three-fourths of our thought and energy in winning bread and clothes and shelter. Yet we have longings and outreachings of the spirit which these earthly comforts cannot satisfy. Is the mere keeping alive worth all the effort expended upon it? Is it not the lure of some undiscovered secret, some unrealized satisfaction, that after all gives life its zest and excitement? The pagans in their loneliness spoke of Mother Earth and sought to find rest by laying weary heads upon her ample breast. But humanity has never found much comfort in the thought. For if "Mother Earth" had been a true word, if our home is here amidst the years, then the red dawn would have touched men as does the kindling of a hearth fire, the mountains would have seemed the massive walls of a garden, and the stars would have uttered in their own grand way the message that twinkles in the lamplight of a cottage window. But this is not so. Man is homeless in the dawn; the mountains give not comfortable shelter but hurting aspiration; and who can stand under the star-fires without feeling the heart aching to take the endless road to which they call? We are strangers on the earth.

Nor is this restlessness of the heart, this loneliness of the soul the peculiar experience of those who have met unusual frustration and failure. Amid the deepest satisfactions to which great souls have won their way, there is the pain of longing and the unvoiced cry for some higher fulfillment. Surely it was not a defeated man who could say, "Thy statutes have been my songs in the house of my pilgrimage. I have remembered thy name, O Lord, in the night, and have kept thy law." Yet it was he who said, "I am a stranger in the earth. . . . My soul breaketh for the longing that it hath unto thy judgments at all times." It was the man who had climbed the heights of spiritual victory who said, "I go unto the Father." And all through that perfect life in perfect labor writ, one feels the homesickness of his supernal soul.

The deepest satisfactions of life beget the deepest longings. Hearing a great symphony, or looking at a breath-takingly beautiful sunset, or feeling the impact of a wonderfully balanced life, gives us joy and some sense of peace; but it also awakens infinite outreaches, calling us above and beyond our petty concerns, and shining on us some glimmer of the far-off lights of home.

The tenderest human love in all its kindly comradeship is a haven in which the ships of desire find rest, but it is also a harbor from which they set sail for the calling deeps. The greatest lover is never the mere sensualist, who knows no rapture but that induced by recurrent physical contact. His love soon palls of its own excess, knowing as it does no spiritual enrichment. He casts off one love and seeks another, unwilling to acknowledge that the failure lies in his own refusal to respond to the divine urgings of his heart toward higher attainment; and ultimately, persisting in his carnality, he turns on himself in disgust and is eaten away in his finest part until in reality he is little more than an animal. No, the greatest lover is the idealist who is stirred by the beauty and ecstasy of a great union to higher attainment. Thus Robert Browning is stirred by his love for Elizabeth to write great poems; and Dante who only worshipped Beatrice from afar is inspired to write *The Divine Comedy*. Thus musicians have been inspired to write great music, builders to build great buildings, artists to paint great paintings. Thus every husband who knows a great union in his home is inspired to go out and earn a livelihood for his loved ones; and the greater the love the greater nobility is inspired in him.

Yet which lover was ever satisfied? Indeed infinite desire begets infinite capacity, and one must, once the higher road is taken, strive ever onward and upward toward the ultimate.

St. Catherine said, "Care not to present a finished work to God who is infinite love and demands of thee only infinite desire." We should be glad of the challenge this unfinished world offers to unlimited attainment. Though the small tasks are necessary and to the right-minded person there is joy in the doing of them, we must not confine ourselves to work that can be finished, for it will usually be too small to feed the hungry spirit of us. If one ever fulfilled his fondest dreams he would have nothing to work for, nothing to stimulate him and keep him alive.

How many times have little boys, looking up with adoring eyes, said to their fathers, "Daddy, when I grow up I want to be just like you." But how foolish the father who, warmed to the core by such childish devotion, is so unselfcritical as not to blush for his shortcomings happily unknown to the child! so weak willed as not to resolve and strive to be a better man that such devotion can be continued and better deserved! Just as the child needs, indeed as we all need heroes to inspire us; so heroes need the trust and confidence of their followers to keep them ever steady, ever growing, ever responsive and alive to new fields of spiritual conquest.

If we set ourselves only goals that can be grasped, how can the grasping be significant to us? "Man's reach should exceed his grasp, or what's a heaven for?" asked Browning. No, we must ever enlarge our horizons, for "where the soul can find no room to expand, contraction sets in."

This continual craving for what lies beyond, for what we cannot see but only sense, for what we cannot know but do, despite all material distracting evidences, in our most secret hearts most persistently believe—this in reality is the soul's affinity to the divine, its loyalty to its ultimate goal of full union with God, its faithfulness to its destiny. St. Paul said, "I count myself not to have laid hold: but one thing I do, forgetting the things which are behind and stretching forward to the things which are before, I press on toward the goal unto the prize of the high calling of God in Christ Jesus."

Those who have seen the lights of home tell us that the journey is not futile; that it does not end at last in the shoreless abyss of nothingness. The one who sounded life's deepest depths and scaled its highest peaks, the pioneer of life, the expert in human experience—what does he say? That life is a journey: "If ye loved me, ye would have rejoiced, because I go unto the Father: for the Father is greater than I. . . . Let not your heart be troubled: ye believe in God, believe also in me. In my Father's house are many mansions: if it were not so, I would have told you. I go to prepare a place for you."

Sometimes even you and I in angel-haunted hours have pierced the veil and touched abiding reality. Those ideals that woo us and humble us and hurt us seem to say, "You are a stranger here. You must not settle down; you must prepare for a home to which you go." In one of Mr. Ervine's plays, *The Ship,* old Mrs. Thurlow says, "To me, the most wonderful thing in the world is not the young man beginning life with ideals —we all do that—but the old man dying with them undiminished."[13] It is not Jacob in his youth seeing the angel traffic of the heavenly ladder that tells the glory of life. It is Jacob, grown old and rich, with flocks and herds about him, and still by Jabbok's brim wrestling with God's angel.

Have you ever read the biography of Edward Wilson, the naturalist and saint, who twice went with the hero, Captain Scott, on Antarctic expeditions?[14] From the last expedition they did not return. In the weary wastes of the polar barrier searchers found their bodies with arms locked in an embrace. Realizing what was to happen Wilson had, before his rebirth, written a message to his wife. Listen to its deep soul meanings: "God be with you in your trouble, my dear, when I have gone. I leave this life in absolute faith and the happy belief that if God wishes you to wait long it will be for some purpose. All is best for those that love God, and O my Ory, we have loved Him all our lives. All is well. We struggled to the end and we have nothing to regret. The barrier has beaten us though we got to the Pole. My beloved wife, these are small things; life itself is a small thing to me now, but my love for you is forever a part of our love for God. I do not cease to pray that you may be filled with the knowledge of His will. My only regret is to leave you to struggle alone, but I may be coming to you by a quicker way. Dad's little compass and Mother's little comb and looking glass are in my pocket. Your little Testament and Prayer Book will be

in my hand or in my breast pocket when the end comes.
. . . All is well."

Those who, like Wilson, open their hearts and minds to a great and wonderful love know that life in space-time is a journey and that rebirth is not an end, but a beginning. Secure in their faith, they build more richly here and at rebirth go forward more adequately prepared for the life that is to come.

As Robertson of Brighton used to say, "There are men in whom the resurrection begun makes the resurrection credible." The spirit of the risen Saviour works in them. They have risen above the narrowness of life and all that is petty and selfish; they have risen above self; they have risen with Christ. They have become the symphony of the faith.

PART THREE

Faith and the Works

I feel in myself the future life. I am like a forest once cut down; the new shoots are stronger and livelier than ever. I am rising, I know, toward the sky. The sunshine is on my head. The earth gives me its generous sap, but heaven lights me with the reflection of unknown worlds.

You say the soul is nothing but the resultant of the bodily powers. Why, then, is my soul more luminous when my bodily powers begin to fail? Winter is on my head, but the eternal spring is in my heart. I breathe at this hour the fragrance of the lilies, the violets and the roses, as at twenty years. The nearer I approach the end, the plainer I hear around me the immortal symphonies of the worlds which invite me. It is marvelous, yet simple. It is a fairy tale, and it is history.

For half a century I have been writing my thoughts in prose and in verse; history, philosophy, drama, romance, tradition, satire, ode and song; I have tried all. But I feel I have not said the thousandth part of what is in me. When I go down to the grave I can say, like many others, 'I have finished my day's work.' But I cannot say, 'I have finished my life.' My day's work will begin again the next morning. The tomb is not a blind alley; it is a thoroughfare. It closes on the twilight, opens on the dawn.

VICTOR HUGO

I showed my friend the empty tomb and set before him the written record that Jesus was indeed alive.

But he did not believe.

"For," said he, "I have looked into your heart and I find it selfish, ambitious, proud. I see that it is envious and grudging. No, your Christ is dead forever more!"

Then I saw my friend in need and I forgot my proofs. I gave up my argument and began to share what I had with him. I sought out the bruises that life had left upon his soul, and in some strange fashion I became a minister for their healing.

And then he believed!

"For," said he, "I know he lives in you. Yes, your Christ liveth!"

CHAPTER VII

❧

Through Faith to the Works and to the Victory

IN one sense the most skeptical, the most analytical of us know that we will never die. After our days in space-time are completed, we will live on in the conditions we have created. No one leaves the earth as he found it. Think of the difference Jesus made —he split the calendar! How different was life after him! The world has Christmas and it has Easter; it has an experience of God in life for its inspiration; it has a vision of the person as the Divine, of man as big enough for a free world. All of us influence life for better or for worse. We know at this moment that we live on in the good and evil we do.

Hitler is still living and will live on for a long time in human misery. The malignancy he and those who encouraged him engendered is still at work in hundreds of millions of lives where normal development and satisfactions are displaced by sorrow, bereavement, frustration, hatred, homelessness, hopelessness and utter misery. Indeed the evil that men do lives after them; it cannot be buried with their bones.

But it is equally true that the good that men do lives after they have finished their days in space-time. Generations long gathered into history have made us rare bequests. We do not have to build society anew in each generation. Though our cities may be poorly planned and inadequate, yet they have their parks, playgrounds, libraries, museums, colleges, universities, churches—and all the other gifts in which people who have lived in the past live on endlessly in the blessings of those that follow. Though there is a snake belt in Columbus, Ohio, there is also a Central Community House. Though the evil of past generations has bequeathed to us blighted personalities, broken homes, cleavages between labor and management, and wars— yet good also was bequeathed to us in the Bible, in the Christmas and Easter stories, in the glorious history of the Living Church, in public schools, in hospitals, private homes and other noble institutions of human love.

Jesus lives in every home where there is true love, in every incentive that enriches life, in our very way of life with its democratic ideal. Elizabeth Fry lives in every effort to improve prisons. Lincoln lives in every effort to unshackle the enslaved; Watt and Stephenson live every time steam gives us power. Gutenberg still lives in every printed word. Marconi lives in every radio. Lister, Pasteur and a vast galaxy of deathless men and women live in every life saved by modern science. Homer lives in every poet; David in every singer; Ruth in every lover; Mary in every great mother; Joseph in every great father. And all of us know that their work is not finished but must be continued in us.

Do you remember reading of the last days of Socrates? Crito, his friend, asked, "How do you want to be buried?" And Socrates said, "Conduct a funeral according to conventionality, but remember you cannot bury Socrates."

Isn't it interesting that the burial place of Moses was unknown? Though we are told in the 34th Chapter of Deuteronomy that he was buried "in the valley in the land of Moab over against Bethpeor," in the same passage we read, "but no man knoweth of his sepulchre unto this day." Naturally Moses himself could not be put into the ground. He lives in the people to whom he gave a soul. He lives in every Jew, he lives in every Christian, for all of them have been touched by the spirit of one who "endured as seeing Him who is invisible." He lives in the law and in every lawyer and judge; he lives wherever men govern themselves by law for the glory of God and the good of all.

Though it is not given to each of us to leave as great a heritage as that left us by Lincoln, or by Moses, or by Jesus, every one of us can in his life plant seed that shall grow to trees bearing fruit or giving shade. Once I helped my father plant peach trees, and I asked him, "Do you expect to live to eat peaches off of these trees?" His reply was thrilling and a great message for a boy to ponder: "I don't know, but it makes no difference. All my life I've eaten fruit from trees others have planted. So I want to plant trees that will bear fruit for those who live beyond my days."

In this sense we all know we live on. We cannot deny it. Why do we refuse to face it? Those young people who spend one weekend after another drinking beer and wasting time, or who insist on making a plaything out of what God means to be holy; those of us who go on being vegetables when we really have the soul of the divine; those of us who have no interest but money and pleasure that smother the soul and keep us from our true nature; those of us who make up a nation that spends 60% of its income on war and war preparation and pennies on peace, a paltry 1.8% on education, and a mere .4% on religion and finding the secret of life;—all combine to make up a bequest to the future of sick personalities, broken homes, child crime, tyranny, the loss of self government, and endless war in the world.

To those who lived before us there is nothing we can give; from those who live now and will live after us there is nothing we can withhold. Whatever we make of ourselves goes into making up the wealth of the future in individual life and in the collective whole.

When my days in the physical body are finished and my ashes are returned to the good earth, I beg those who love me not to put up a memorial stone. I want no plaque or tablet anywhere, for I shall have living memorials in whatever influence for good God has seen fit to make through me on the lives of little children, young people, grown men and women. And because I know that the good I have omitted to do will be a testimony against me and perhaps unwittingly result in blighted lives, I shall ever strive to do more and more of the portion of God's work that comes to my hand.

Just as we as individuals live on in the work we do, so each family lives on in its children. The parents' attitudes will mark the child's personality, help set the goals he will seek. The methods the child employs to achieve his goals will determine the quality of immortality of the parents. Whatever he is is a fulfillment of their life and an immediate source of satisfaction to them. What he is is their present immortality. They live on in him. Every response he makes to life will be a recollection of them. His appreciations, his love will reflect them. The quality of his character is the spiritual checking account they established. The size of it and how long it endures is a testimony of the life they lived, of the quality of their devotions and the measure of their faith.

Timothy, one of the leaders of the early church, is a thrilling illustration of this immortality. Paul spoke about the unfeigned faith that was in him, saying it had dwelt first in his grandmother and then in his mother. The faith of his grandmother and his mother achieved immortality in Timothy.

Similarly, what we as Americans do today will achieve its immortality in the United States of tomorrow. What we invest in terms of education, housing, and providing equality of opportunity for all will be what we will reap. Immortality of the nation depends upon the quality of its people, their vision and their love.

America split the atom, but though she is trying to feed the hungry she has not succeeded too well. The nation that can split the atom ought to learn to provide equality of opportunity for all. A nation that is embarrassed with abundance ought to learn how to share that abundance so that all of God's children will have enough.

America will only live on in future generations as she lives fully enough in each passing generation. What is done in the present is always prophetic of what is to be in the future, in individuals, in families, in communities, and in nations.

The writer of Hebrews is sure that we are not alone. He tells us that Moses endured as "seeing him who is invisible." He speaks of a man who by a stroke of favor found himself within reach of a great throne, a place of leadership in a mighty empire. But Moses turned away from that to become the leader and inspiration of a band of run-away slaves. He did the daring thing, even though he was to know hardship and poverty and the base ingratitude of those for whom he had forsaken all. By the sheer power of his own soul he had to communicate courage and hope to his despairing followers. Above all, he was constrained to see them betray the religious faith for the freedom and destiny of which he had led them forth in search of a new home. And now as the writer of the Hebrews looks back over the romance and heroism of that consecrated life, he sees not one thing in Moses' environment or in his comradeship that can account for his courage. What made him go on? Where was the hidden power? From what secret spring did he refresh and energize his soul? Moses endured, concludes the writer, "as seeing him who is invisible." He lived and acted as if he saw that which cannot be seen—and yet that which can be so richly known. He did such great work because *he was not alone.*

Can we also endure? That is the question we face. You who have gone through a convention, made your resolves—can you endure? We who have inherited a rich social order with the democratic ideal in it—can we endure? So much of life in its highest aspirations and outreaches comes to just that—enduring when every wind is contrary and every voice cries, "Fool"; enduring in the face of the violent opposition of those who would make life static and stagnant; harder still, enduring when there are no visible antagonists against whom to take the field, but when the whole atmospheric pressure is secular and skeptical; enduring when every dear hope of one's heart has met apparent defeat; enduring when one's own mind doubts and questions.

Endurance is not just tenacity or pride or stubbornness. Strength for it comes from the soul's vision of the invisible God. Joan of Arc is sure she hears voices; but she is burned at the stake without witnessing the triumph of her highest hopes. Savonarola consecrates himself to the moral redemption of Florence, and his antagonists cause him to be killed in the name of the God he loves and serves; so that he does not see the fruition of his dreams. Tyndale gives the people of England the Bible in their own tongue, and he is hounded like a felon until at last his body is brutally dishonored and his ashes thrown to the winds. John Bunyan is thirteen years in Bedford jail because he gives testimony to his soul's knowledge of God, and he does not know he will lift the world to simpler and sublimer ideas of the eternal. These people endured, and millions like unto them,—nameless, unknown—have endured as if they saw the invisible.

There is no other way in the high enterprises of the spirit. Faith always means living as if something were true in order to make it true. By an imperial act of will we have to put meaning into life if we are going to find meaning there. If we just drift along with the eye alert to catch here and there some sign of life's significance, we will not find it. Life will be an idle tale, a part played upon the stage. But if we say, "I believe there is meaning and purpose, noble and beautiful and exacting, at the hidden heart of life," and begin to respond to that purpose, then we shall find it. There is no other way. As we must plant the acorn to find the universal forces that produce the oak, so we, by faith, must put moral purpose and passion into life to find the fellowship of that divine will at the soul of life. In a beautiful parable, Gilbert Frensen says, "I sowed my enemy's field with corn that God might continue to exist." That is a deep insight. He did not create God by his act of forviging love, but he found the reality of God for his own soul by doing it. He put meaning into life and found life filled with meanings, spiritual and eternal. Faith is not a thing one loses; it is the thing, consciously or unconsciously, we keep shaping our lives by.

When we seek the ends of love and goodness, disciplined and guided by intelligence, there comes the conviction that we are not alone. Indeed, we find that such ends are not ours at all, but that we have entered into the mighty purpose of the universe. There is born a sense of companionship and, in the hearts of those most complete in their consecration, a peace that passes all understanding. Passionately putting meaning into life, they find meaning there. The great support and inspiration of love and sacrifice and high heroism is to believe that those qualities which we find here and there in human souls are not just broken, stray beams of light, but direct rays from one mighty sun. All you have to do to believe in God is to believe that all that is highest and most humane in yourself—love and truth—is not only in yourself but also in the universe. That belief is of personal validity and of cosmic significance as well. As a bit of electrical energy in a piece of magnetized steel is a token of the totality of electrical energy in the cosmos, so the love and goodness of the human heart are not isolated phenomena—they betoken One who is the soul and source of all goodness and love. As man tunnels up through earth's dark and damp toward the stars, he hears the tools of a master worker digging down from the upper side. He hears and takes heart. He knows that the visions of his soul are valid. Life is no accident. Somewhere it has abiding significance. And man endures as seeing him who is invisible.

And so, strengthened by the vision, instead of wasting himself away in repining, each man adds his energies to those of other people to do the world's work. The more he does the more he can do. The more he gives in love the more he has. That is Christ's teaching, and it is infallible. Each one of us, if he will examine his heart, knows that this is true in his own limited experience, that whenever he has hurt anyone else he has hurt himself more. Why then torture ourselves with denial? The more one acknowledges and acts on the good in him, the more the good grows and the wider its influence is felt. The possibilities are exciting, and limitless if all take part. And more and more must soon take part if the world as we know it is to be saved from annihilation. This then is the call—the call to each and every one to come to the second birth, to spiritual awakening. Not some vague time in the future—procrastination defeats us—but now, now in the indestructible present, we may receive the sacrament of the instantaneous moment.

NOTES AND REFERENCES

[1] From *Masterpieces of Religious Verse,* edited by James Dalton Morrison, Harper & Bros., New York and London, 1948, p. 384.

[2] From *Remember April,* compiled by Margaret E. Burton, the Womans Press, New York, 1941, p. 53.

[3] "My Hereafter" by Juanita de Long, from *The World's Great Religious Poetry,* edited by Caroline Miles Hill, Macmillan Co., New York, 1926, p. 704.

[4] "Release" by Jean Grigsby Paxton, from *Remember April, op. cit.,* p. 14.

[5] Part of this material on suffering and the problem of evil was used in the author's book, *How the Church Grows,* published by Harper & Bros., 1947.

[6] "The Great Wager" by G. A. Studdert-Kennedy, from *The Master of of Men, Quotable Poems About Jesus,* compiled by Thomas Curtis Clark, published by Richard R. Smith, Inc., New York, 1930, p. 20-21.

[7] From *Remember April, op. cit.,* p. 44. Acknowledgment given to Charles W. Gilkey for quotation from an Easter sermon.

[8] "If This Were My Last Speech" by Robert A. Millikan, from *Motive* magazine, published by the Methodist Student Movement, Nashville, Tennessee, April, 1950, p. 6.

[9] I am indebted to Dr. Boynton Merrill of the First Congregational Church of Columbus, Ohio, for some of the ideas on faith in this chapter, and to Dr. George Buttrick of the Madison Avenue Presbyterian Church of New York for ideas about mystery.

[10] From *Masterpieces of Religious Verse, op. cit.,* pp. 73-74.

[11] From *Remember April, op. cit.,* p. 21. Permission from the Christian Century Pulpit, Chicago, for quotation from the sermon *Vigil in the Heart.*

[12] The writer has been unable to trace the authorship of the idea of which this is a restatement.

[13] *The Ship,* by St. John G. Ervine, The Macmillan Co., New York, 1922, Act I, p. 16.

[14] See *Edward Wilson of the Antarctic,* by George Seaver, London, J. Murray, 1933.